Give yourself a sticker when you've finished each page.

Use these stickers on the progress chart in the middle of the book.

    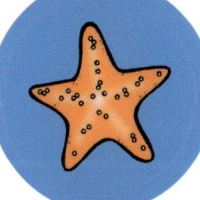 

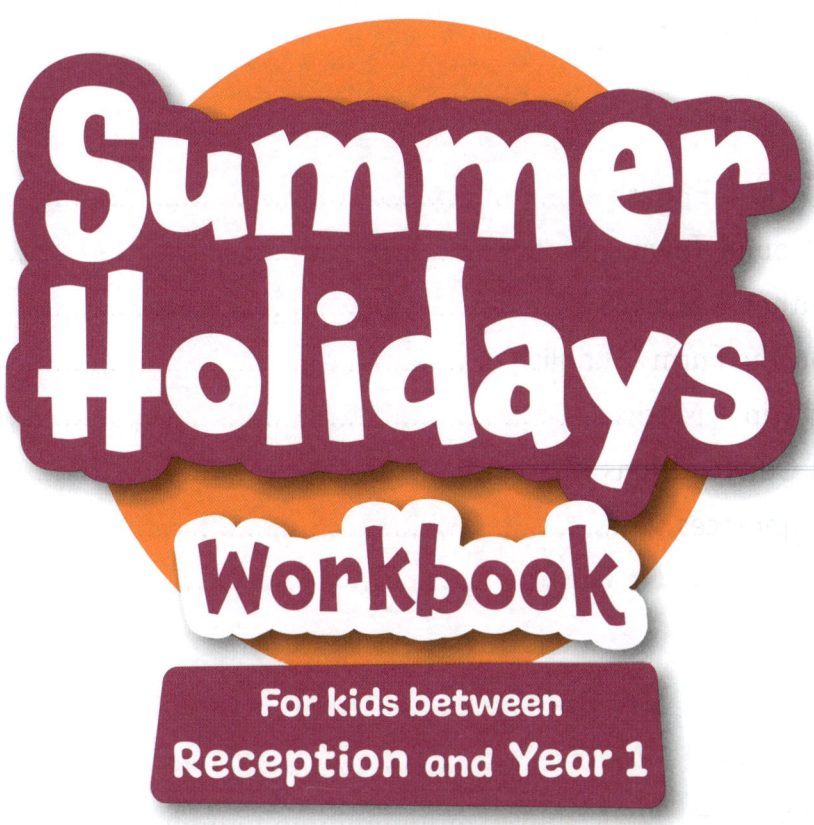

Summer Holidays Workbook

For kids between Reception and Year 1

This book is full of exciting practice that kids can really get stuck into over the summer holidays!

It's got activities and puzzles for all the main school subjects, matched to the Early Years Curriculum. Plus there are lots of colourful stickers.

And it's a CGP book, so it's more fun than a frog riding a unicycle!

Contents

☑ Use the tick boxes to help keep a record of which pages you've done.
Update your **Sticker Progress Map** once you've completed a full week.

Sticker Progress Map 28

Week 1

- ☑ Camping Trip – English 2
- ☑ A Walk Around Town – Maths 3
- ☑ Wild Weather – Science 4
- ☑ Sounds on the Farm – English 5
- ☑ Shopping Trip – Maths 6
- ☑ Colourful Combinations – Art 7
- ☑ Daisy's Differences 8
- ☑ **Challenge – Nature Bingo** 9

Week 2

- ☑ Professor Pyramid – Maths 10
- ☑ Animal Sounds – Music, English 11
- ☑ Lola's Loot – English 12
- ☑ Brave Knights – Maths 13
- ☑ Town or Country? – Geography 14
- ☑ Fun at the Park – English 15
- ☑ Alien Art 16
- ☑ **Challenge – Painting Pebbles** 17

Week 3

- ☑ Who Lives Here? – Science 18
- ☑ Make a Splash – English 19
- ☑ The Flower Garden – Maths 20
- ☑ Scenes from the Past – History 21
- ☑ Arthur's Walk – English 22
- ☑ Sweet Treats – Maths 23
- ☑ Diving Dot-to-Dot 24
- ☑ **Challenge – Test Your Talents** 25

Week 4

- [ ] Odds and Evens – Maths 26
- [ ] The Busy Bee – English 27
- [ ] Arty Shapes – Art, Maths 30
- [ ] Sorting Toys – Maths, Art 31
- [ ] Different Places – Geography 32
- [ ] A Dog's Life – English 33
- [ ] Find the Missing Piece 34
- [ ] **Challenge – Colourful Celery** **35**

Week 5

- [ ] Building Blocks – Maths 36
- [ ] Ordering Pictures – Science, Maths 37
- [ ] Colourful Creatures – English 38
- [ ] Starry Sky – Maths 39
- [ ] Playing at Gran's House – English 40
- [ ] Toys Through Time – History, Maths 41
- [ ] Pudding Patterns 42
- [ ] **Challenge – Peppermint Creams** **43**

Week 6

- [ ] Season Scramble – Geography, Science 44
- [ ] How Many Raindrops? – Maths 45
- [ ] Animal Escape – English 46
- [ ] Scavenger Hunt – Science 47
- [ ] Running Rhymes – English 48
- [ ] Party Time! – Maths 49
- [ ] Dino Matching 50
- [ ] **Challenge – Handprint Fish** **51**

Answers 52
Summer Reading Challenge 58
Certificate 59
My Summer Highlight 60

Published by CGP

Editors: Claire Boulter, Helen Clements, Josie Gilbert, Paul Jordin, Julie Wakeling

With thanks to Juliette Green, Catherine Heygate and Glenn Rogers for the proofreading.

With thanks to Alice Dent for the copyright research.

All activities, crafts and recipes in this book should be carried out under the supervision of a responsible adult, who should ensure appropriate safety precautions are taken. CGP cannot be held responsible for any type of loss, damage or injury to individuals resulting from the content of this book.

ISBN: 978 1 83774 218 9

Cover and Graphics used throughout the book © www.edu-clips.com

Printed by Elanders Ltd, Newcastle upon Tyne.

Text, design, layout and original illustrations © Coordination Group Publications Ltd. (CGP) 2025
All rights reserved.

CGP Broughton House, Griffin Street, Broughton-in-Furness, Cumbria. LA20 6HH
CGP c/o Elanders GmbH, Anton-Schmidt-Str. 15, 71332 Waiblingen, GERMANY. info@elanders-germany.com

Photocopying this book is not permitted, even if you have a CLA licence.
Extra copies are available from CGP with next day delivery • 0800 1712 712 • www.cgpbooks.co.uk

Hints for Helpers

- This book contains **6 weeks'** worth of **questions**, **puzzles** and **activities**.
- The pages recap important content from **Reception**, and include some extra challenges and puzzles to help prepare for **Year 1**.
- Each week is made up of **8 pages**:

There are **6 pages** of questions each week. Each week covers a mix of **subjects**.

The **7th page** of each week is a **fun puzzle** that isn't linked to a particular subject.

There's a **reward sticker** for every page, which can be found on the **sticker sheet**.

The **final page** of each week is an **activity** to try at home.

- The middle two pages are a **progress map**:

Once each week is done, use the number stickers from the sticker sheet to update the **progress map**. Once all the number stickers are in place, **complete** the progress map.

Let's go — Ready to get cracking? Let's go!

Camping Trip

Summer Holidays — Week 1

1 **Read** the **story** about a camping trip. **Circle** the things in the **picture** that are mentioned in the **story**.

The tent is near a tree.

The moon is bright.

An owl hoots.

A fox looks at the owl.

2 Bart is on a camping trip. **Find** each item on Bart's **packing list** in the picture and **colour** it in the colour given in the list.

pink sleeping bag

red camping chair

green tent

brown socks

Brilliant work! Pop a sticker on the page.

A Walk Around Town

Maths

Dinah has **numbered** the places in her town showing what **order** she visited them in.

Put a moon 🌙 sticker on the place Dinah visited **last**.

Put a sun ☀ sticker on the place Dinah visited **before** the **park**.

Dinah spots that some of the houses on her street don't have numbers. **Fill in** the correct numbers on the **houses**.

Well done! Now you can choose a sticker.

Summer Holidays — Week 1

Science

Wild Weather

Draw lines to **match** each person to the place they are dressed for.

Draw what the **weather** is like where you are today. Then **circle** the items you would wear outside.

Things are looking sunny! Go and find a sticker.

Sounds on the Farm

1 **Read** the **sound** on each **hay bale**. **Colour** the **picture** below it that contains that **sound**.

or   ee   ai

2 Complete each word by choosing the correct **letter pair** from the **clouds**.

Clouds: ow, ee, er   ar, oa

sh……p

g……t

b……n

c…….

f……m……

Farm-tastic! Time to give yourself a sticker.

Summer Holidays — Week 1

Shopping Trip

Circle the correct shopper.

Who has **more** peppers ?

Who has **less** bread ?

Now try this — There are **six differences** between the cake displays. **Circle** the differences on the display on the right.

Q: Why did the cake visit the doctor? A: It was feeling crumby!

Colourful Combinations

Colour each paint splat in the colour written **underneath** it.

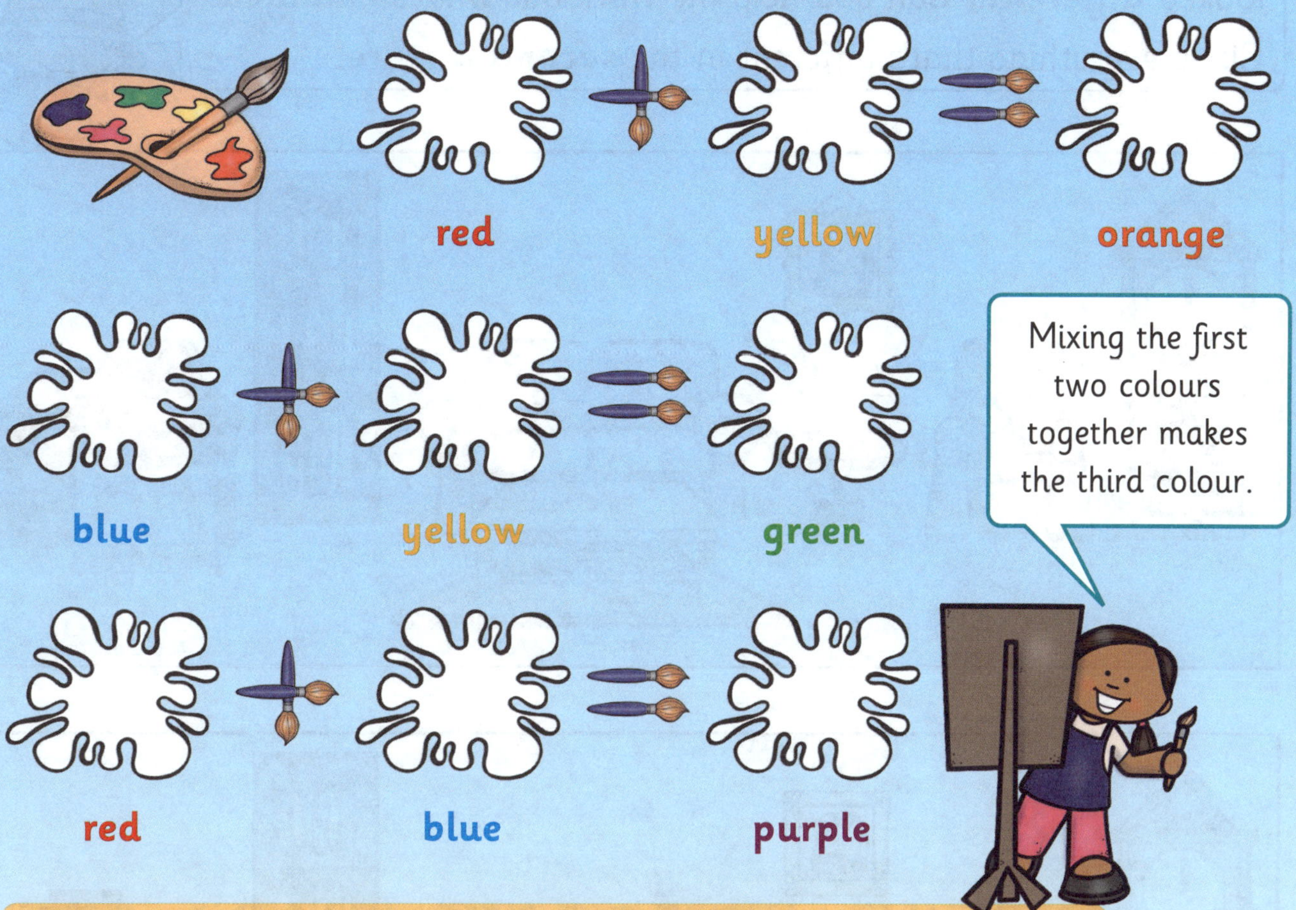

red   yellow   orange

blue   yellow   green

Mixing the first two colours together makes the third colour.

red   blue   purple

Use the colours from the paint splats to **colour** in the **rainbow**.

Great job on this page! You've earned a new sticker.

Summer Holidays — Week 1

Daisy's Differences

I'm Detective Daisy. When I got home today, my living room looked **different**. Can you help me work out what's **changed**? Circle everything that's different in the **second picture**.

How many differences did you find? Count the differences and write your answer in the box.

Amazing detective work! Now track down a sticker.

Nature Bingo

Week 1 Challenge

Go to your **garden** or local **park** and see what you can find. Draw a **line** through each thing you spot. Can you find them all?

tree	squirrel	worm	bird
bee	log	ant	leaf
flower	rock	ladybird	web
butterfly	snail	feather	acorn

Summer Holidays — Week 1

Summer Holidays — Week 2

Professor Pyramid

Can you help **Professor Pyramid** sort out his room?

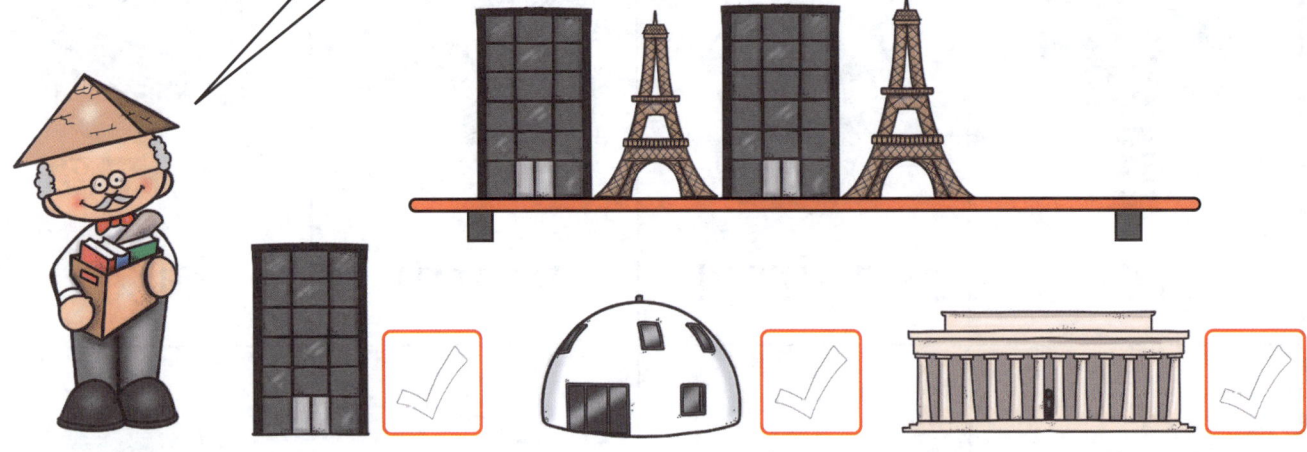

Which **model** should I put on my shelf to carry on the pattern? **Tick** the right answer.

Draw and **colour** the next two buttons in my pattern.

I sorted these toys by **shape**. **Circle** the one that doesn't fit.

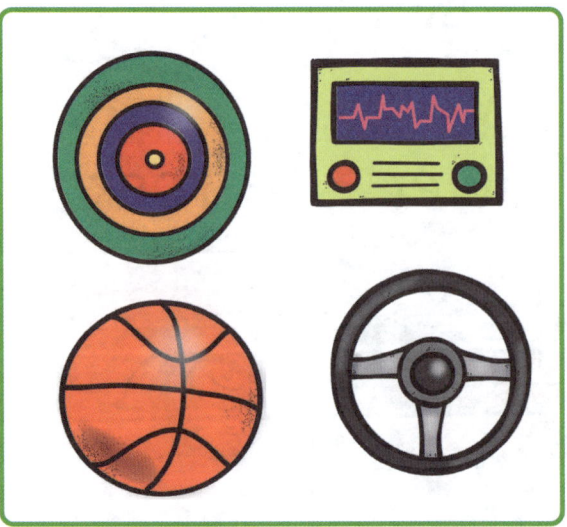

You're looking in great shape! Don't forget to grab your sticker.

Animal Sounds

Music
English

1 Draw a line to match each **animal** to the **noise** it makes.

Can you make each sound?

Quack

Moo

Oink

Ribbit

Sssss

Woof

2 **Colour** in these animals. What **sound** does each one make?

Roarsome job! Make some noise as you choose a sticker.

Summer Holidays — Week 2

English

Lola's Loot

Lola is packing for a **treasure-hunting** trip. Write the **missing letters** to complete each item on her list.

| sh | ch | nk |

dri........    bru........    lun........

The map shows the route Lola's ship will take. **Colour** in the pictures and **write** the correct **missing letters** from the scroll to finish each word.

........ip

si........

ng
ch
sh

........ark

........est

Q: What's a pirate's favourite school subject?   A: Arrrr-t.

Summer Holidays — Week 2

Brave Knights

Maths

Look! The dragons have come for a visit!

How many can you see in the picture? **Write** the **number** in the box.

  flags

  dragons

  towers

  knights

 Well done! Now go on a quest to find your sticker.

Summer Holidays — Week 2

Geography: Town or Country?

Draw **lines** to show whether each item is found in the **town** or the **countryside**.

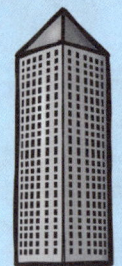

Now try this: Find a way through the **maze** to help Alex the farmer reach her **cows**.

What else might you see in the town or the countryside?

Did you solve the maze? Give yourself a sticker.

Summer Holidays — Week 2

Fun at the Park

English

Read this story about a **trip** to the **park**.

We go to the park.

Ben and Tess are on the swings.

Dad sits on a bench.

We hear a dog bark.

1 What is Dad **sitting on**? Circle the right answer.

  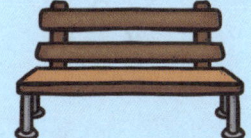 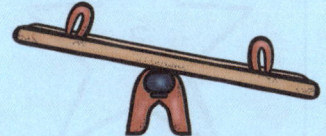

2 Who has a **yellow top**? Tick the right answer.

Dad    Ben    Tess

3 Which **animal** do they hear? Circle the right answer.

What's your favourite thing to do in the park? Draw a picture of it.

Alien Art

Work out the **answer** to each **sum**.

2 + 2 = ☐ = red

4 − 3 = ☐ = blue

3 + 3 = ☐ = green

1 + 4 = ☐ = purple

5 − 3 = ☐ = orange

2 + 1 = ☐ = yellow

Match your **answers** to the **numbers** in the picture.
Colour in the picture using the **colours** next to each **answer**.

You're out of this world! Grab yourself a sticker.

Painting Pebbles

Week 2 Challenge

Let's get crafty! These funky **summer pebbles** will look great on your **windowsill** or in the **garden**.

What you need:

- Large, smooth pebbles
- Poster paint in different colours
- Paintbrushes
- An old plate

1 Start by thinking up a design. You could draw it on paper first.

  **2** Squeeze blobs of the paint colours you need onto the plate.

3 If you want a background colour, paint it on first — like this blue sky.

  **4** Let the first colour dry. Paint on the next colour.

5 Let that dry, and add any final details.

Summer Holidays — Week 2

Summer Holidays — Week 3

Who Lives Here?

Can you help these animals find their way home?

1 Draw lines to **match** each home to the animal that lives there.

2 Ivy the bee is lost! **Draw** along the **path** she should follow to get home.

Think of some other types of animal. Do you know where they live?

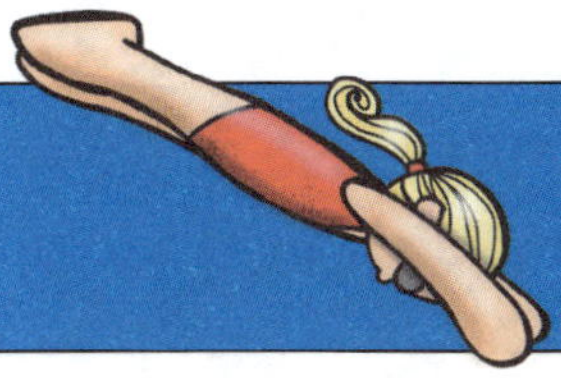

Make a Splash

English

The children are playing in a swimming pool. Draw lines to **match** each **sentence** to the **person** in the picture that it describes.

Gwen jumps in.

Chad floats in a ring.

Zack shivers.

Oliver has armbands.

Liz splashes.

Amber has a hat on.

Now try this — Colour in the picture that contains the **ow** sound.

You're a swimming sensation! Find a sticker to put on the page.

Summer Holidays — Week 3

The Flower Garden

Draw **more** flowers in the garden to make **10 flowers**.

Now try this How many butterflies can you spot on this page? **Colour** in the answer.

Did you know that butterflies taste with their feet?

Summer Holidays — Week 3

Scenes from the Past

History

Izzy has invented a **time machine** and travelled back **500 years**.

1 Look at the town. What can you see that is **different** compared to today?

How did people get around?
How did they get food and water?

2 Izzy goes **inside** a house. What is **different** compared to homes today?

How did people stay warm?
How did they light up their homes?

How do you think people will get around in the future?
Draw a picture showing how you think people will travel.

Great work on this page! Time for another sticker.

Summer Holidays — Week 3

Arthur's Walk

English

Arthur and his friends are going for a walk. They have some **questions** to ask along the way. Can you help **answer** them?

What is sitting by the pond? Colour in the answer.

frog   otter

Which letters are missing from **both** words? Colour in the answer.

hi__   she__

ll   ff

What is not on the bench? Colour in the answer.

dog   hat

scarf   books

Which animal starts with the **r** sound? Colour in the answer.

Fantastic work! Don't forget to grab a sticker.

Sweet Treats

Maths

Cross out **half** of the buns in **each** box.

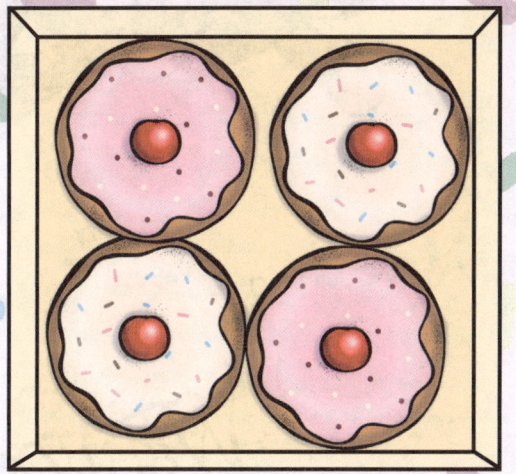
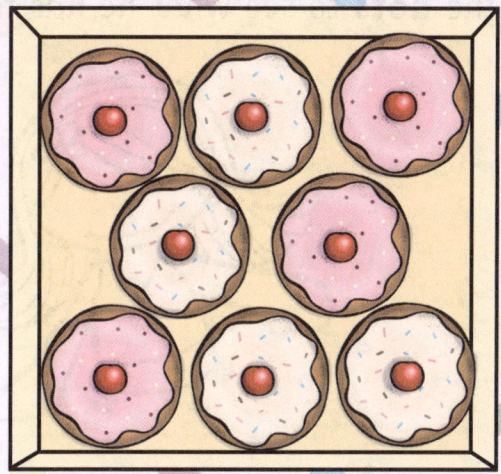

Count the cupcakes on the plate. Now colour in **half** of the cupcakes.

Sweet! Now find yourself a tasty-looking sticker.

Summer Holidays — Week 3

Diving Dot-to-Dot

Dan the diver is exploring the sea. **Join** the **dots** to see what he has found.

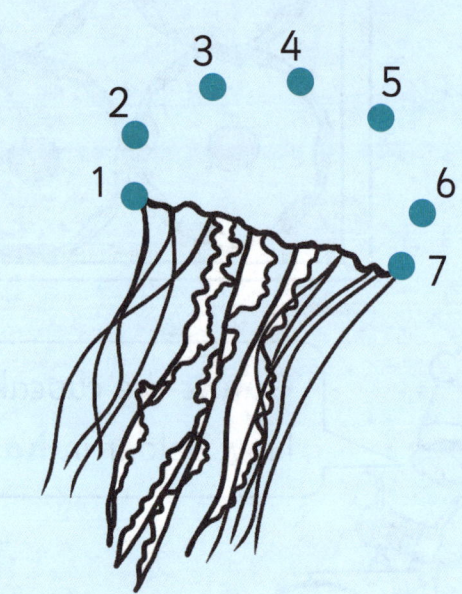

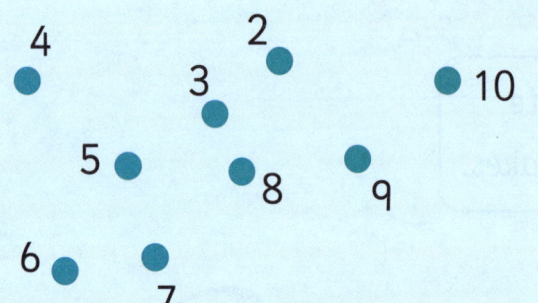

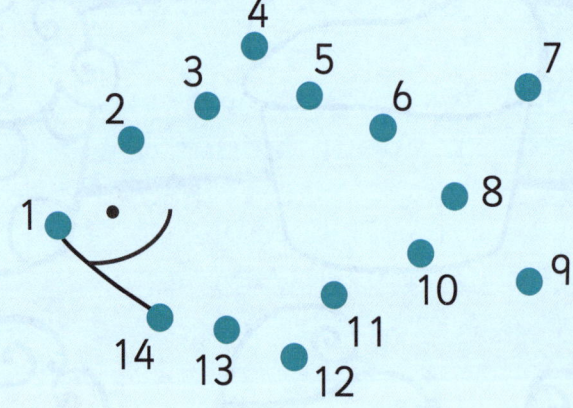

When you've finished joining the dots, **colour** the pictures in.

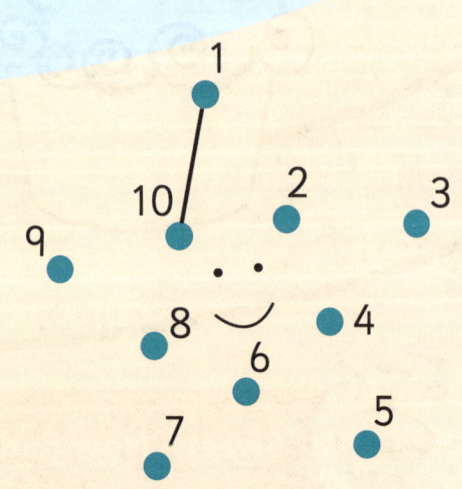

 You did it! Pop your sticker in the circle.

Test Your Talents

Have a go at the challenges below. Try them **more than once** to see if you can **improve**. Write your **best** score in the box.

How long can you stand on one leg? Count how many seconds. ....

Can you balance this book on your head? Count how long you can balance it for. ....

How many times can you bounce a ball against a wall and catch it? Count how many bounces you can do without dropping the ball. ....

How long can you keep a balloon in the air using your hands? Count how many times you tap the balloon without it hitting the ground. ....

Find an outdoor space big enough to jump around. Jump as far as you can — mark your start and finish point so you can measure how far you've jumped. ....

Summer Holidays — Week 4

Week 4 — Maths

Odds and Evens

Beatrice the bird only flies through clouds with **even** numbers on them. Colour in all the clouds she can fly through.

Even numbers end in 2, 4, 6, 8 or 0.

Freddie the frog only hops onto rocks with **odd** numbers on them. Circle all the rocks that he can hop onto.

Now try this — How many people live in your home? Count them out loud and then decide whether that number is even or odd.

Amazing job! Time for a sticker.

The Busy Bee

English

Read this **poem** about a bee.

I am a little buzzing bee,
I float under a big oak tree.
Then I see the sweetest sight —
A pink flower to feed on until night.

What does the bee **feed on**? Circle the right answer.

Which two words **rhyme**? Tick **two** boxes.

bee  night  flower  tree

Now try this — Spot the **differences** between these pictures. Circle each one. There are **five** differences.

 Did you know that bees don't have ears?

Summer Holidays — Week 4

My Holidays Workbook Progress

Help **Pat the Pirate** get to Coral Castle. When you finish a week, find the island that has some **pictures** from **that week**. Add a **sticker** to show the **week number**. When you've got them all, draw a route that visits **all** the islands in turn, from **1** to **6**, and then goes to the **castle**.

Art
Maths

Arty Shapes

Some artists make works of art using **shapes**.

Look at these **pictures**. What do you think each one is? Write down **how many** of each shape are in the picture.

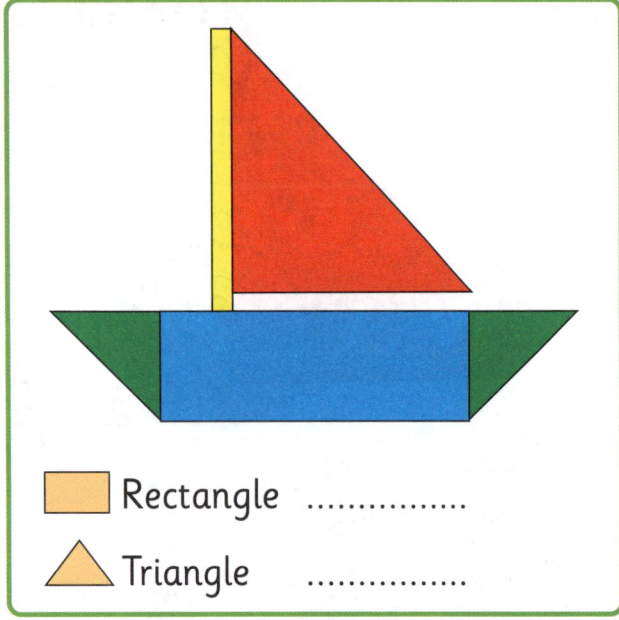

▭ Rectangle ....
△ Triangle ....

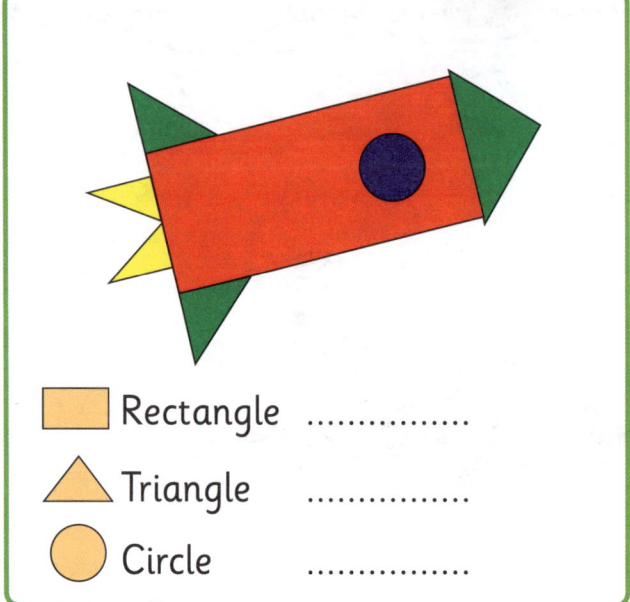

▭ Rectangle ....
△ Triangle ....
◯ Circle ....

Draw a picture of a **house** using **rectangles**, **squares** and **triangles**. Use the dots to help you.

You can change the size and colour of the shapes.

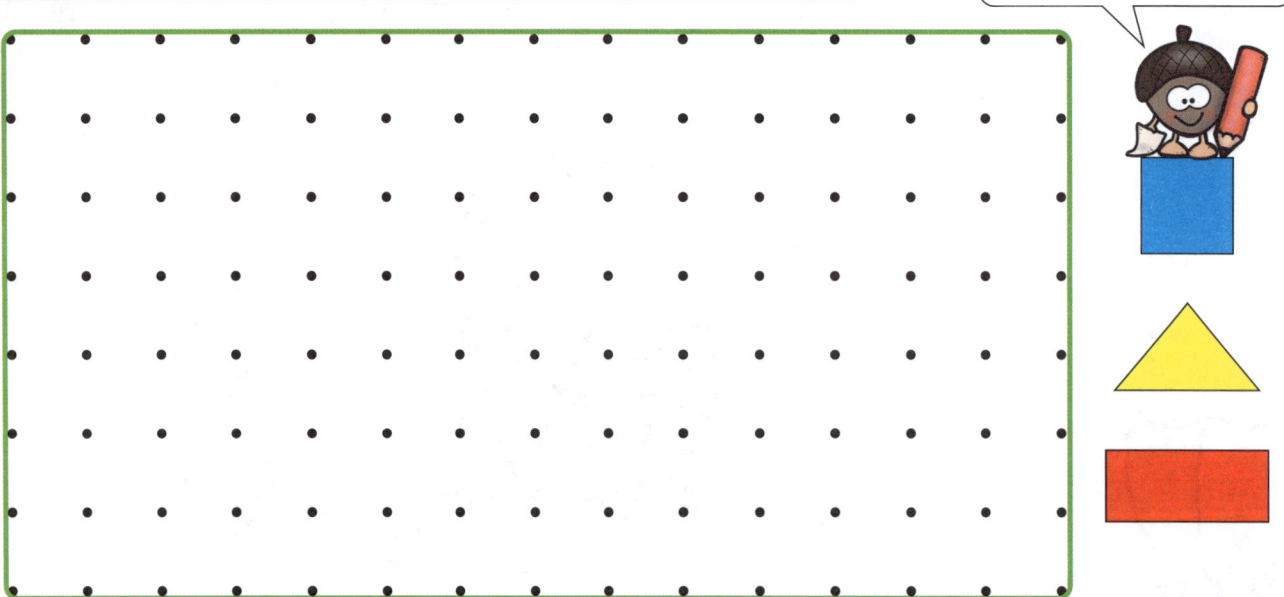

Great job! Time to find that sticker.

Sorting Toys

Maths
Art

Colour in the correct **teddies**.

Colour in the 4th teddy using **red**.

Colour in the 2nd teddy using **blue**.

Draw the items below in the right **order** on the shelf.

2nd   4th   1st   3rd

Incredible work! Go and choose a sticker.

Geography

Different Places

Finn lives in **England** and Pippa lives in **Australia**.

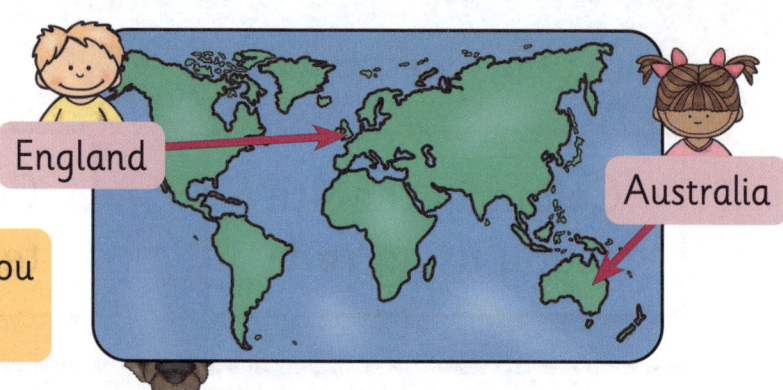

Look at the **map**. What do you know about these **countries**?

Finn and Pippa have sent each other a **photo** of where they live.

England

Australia

1 Which place do you think is **hotter**? Tick a box.

England ☐   Australia ☐

2 Which place is **more built up**? Tick a box.

England ☐   Australia ☐

Now try this — A **platypus** is an Australian animal that has a beak like a duck. There are **six** platypuses hiding on this page. Can you **find** them all? (This one doesn't count.)

Well done! Grab yourself a sticker.

A Dog's Life

English

Help Bob the dog get to the **vet**. Roll a **dice** and **underline** the word you land on, then **read it out**. How **few moves** can you finish in?

woof — jog — wag — fix — van — just — box — wait — wet — mix — wail — vest — jab — wood — wax — joint — visit — wetter — jumps — well

Now try this — Can you name the **parts** of the dog? Choose the right word from the box and **write** it in the label.

leg
tail
ear
chest

 Paw-some job! Find the sticker for this page.

Summer Holidays — Week 4   33

Find the Missing Piece

Each picture below is **missing** a **piece**.
Circle the piece that **completes** each picture.

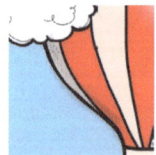 

Draw a picture then cut it up — can you put the pieces back together?

34   Summer Holidays — Week 4

Colourful Celery

Week 4 Challenge

Plants need water to live. You can see how this works with this simple science experiment...

You will need:

a glass of water

a stick of celery

 food colouring

(A stick of celery is a stalk from a celery plant. People eat celery as a vegetable.)

With the help of a grown-up, add a few drops of food colouring to the water.

Then place the cut end of the celery stick into the glass.

After a few hours, you should see that the coloured water has moved up the stem of the celery as the plant takes in water!

Summer Holidays — Week 5

Building Blocks

The trucks are taking bricks to builders on a building site.

On each truck, write down the **number** of bricks it is carrying.
Then write down the **total number** of bricks on each pair of trucks.

Read the information below and then **circle** the correct answer.

I have 3 bricks. I need 8 bricks. How many more bricks do I need?

3   5   7

Draw a wall with 4 bricks, then add 3 more. How many bricks are there?

Ordering Pictures

Number the seasons from **1 to 4** to show what **order** they come in. Spring has been done for you.

Here are some pictures of Leah building a snowman — but they're out of order! **Draw** lines to the numbers to show what **order** they should be in.

 Brr-illiant! Find the sticker for this page.

Colourful Creatures

English

Find the **animal** that matches the **word** on each leaf. Colour each leaf in the **same colour** as the animal on it.

You're a star! Don't forget your sticker!

Starry Sky

Maths

1 **Count** the stars in each window. **Draw** more stars to **double** the number of stars in each window.

2 Look at the **number** of aliens on each planet. **Tick** the set of aliens with **double** this number.

Out of this world! Time to grab a sticker.

Summer Holidays — Week 5

Playing at Gran's House

Nick and his mum visit his gran.

Tick what Nick does when he arrives at Gran's house.

 Frowns  Weeps

 Grins  Sighs

Nick thinks the green car looks fun.

Circle the toy that Nick wants to play with.

Nick will dress up in a crown and a cloak.

What will Nick dress up as? Circle the right answer.

 Can you write a sentence to describe your favourite toy?

Toys Through Time

History
Maths

Nick is trying to work out which of his **toys** his **gran** might have played with when she was **his age**. Draw a **line** from each toy to **Gran** if it is something she might have played with as a **child**.

Now try this Nick is in a toy shop. He has **£10** to spend. **Circle** the **two** toys that Nick can buy and **not** have **any money** left.

Look for two numbers that add up to make 10.

Brilliant job! Don't forget that sticker.

Summer Holidays — Week 5

Pudding Patterns

Finish each row by drawing the **next picture** in the **pattern**.

Great puzzling skills! Time to grab that sticker.

Peppermint Creams

These **tasty sweets** are simple to make — you'll just need a bit of help from a grown up. You could put them in a **jar** or a **box** and give them as a **gift**.

Ingredients:
- 250 grams of royal icing
- A few drops of peppermint extract
- 100 grams of dark chocolate

Equipment:
- Rolling pin
- Small cutter
- Small bowl

Method:

1. Make a well in the middle of the block of icing.

2. Add the peppermint extract.

3. Mix with your hands until it has formed a firm dough.

 4. Roll the dough to about 5 mm thick.

5. Cut out shapes. Put them in the fridge until they harden.

6. Ask a grown up to melt the chocolate.

 7. Dip half of each sweet into the chocolate.

8. Leave until the chocolate sets.

Summer Holidays — Week 6

Season Scramble

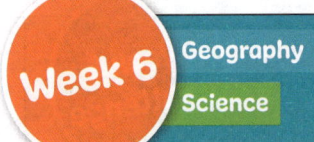

The seasons have got a bit **mixed up** in these pictures.
Circle the part of the picture that doesn't fit the season.

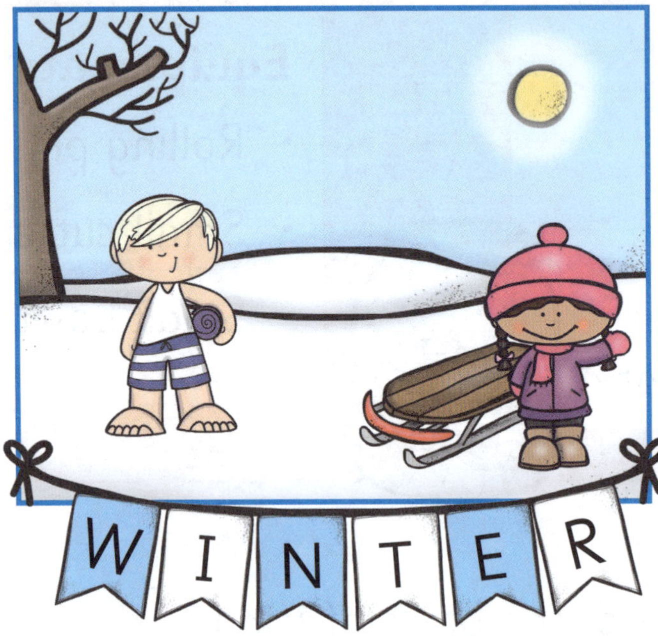

WINTER

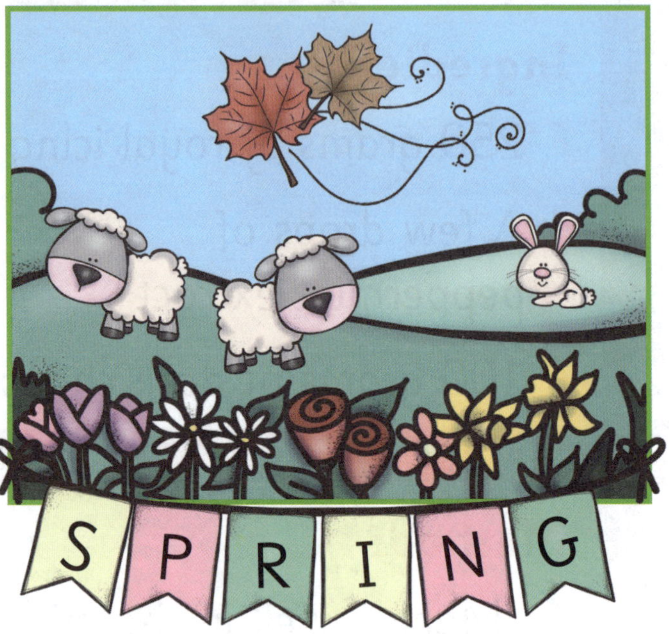

SPRING

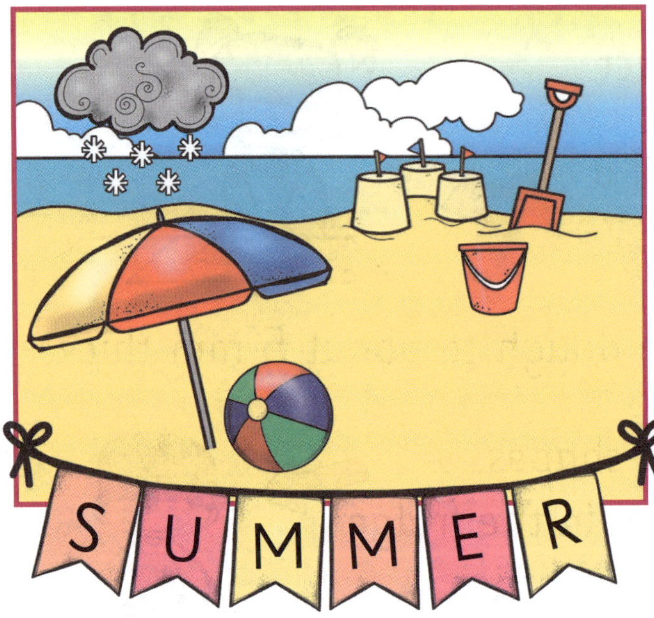

SUMMER

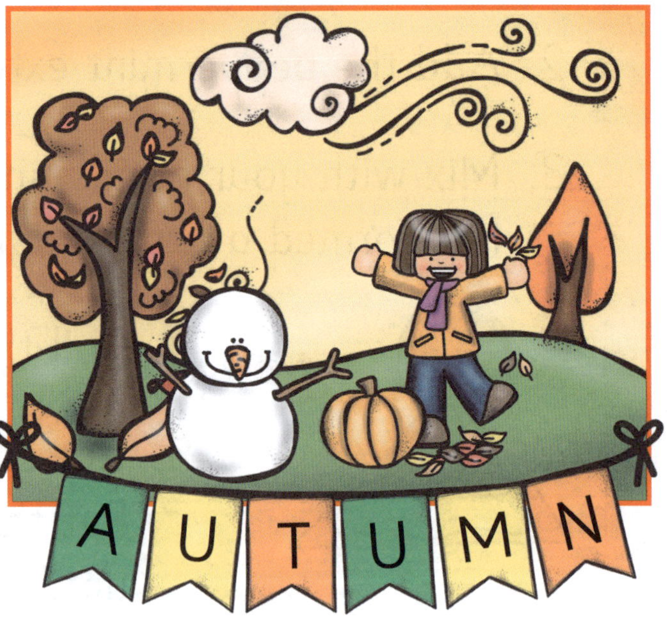

AUTUMN

 Which is your **favourite season**? Draw a **picture** showing what you like about it.

 Spring into action and grab yourself a sticker.

How Many Raindrops?

Maths

It's raining, it's pouring...
Can you count **how many** raindrops are falling from each cloud?

1 **Colour in** the clouds that have an **even number** of raindrops.

2 **Circle** all the clouds that have **fewer than five** raindrops.

Q: What goes up when the rain comes down?   A: An umbrella!

Summer Holidays — Week 6

Animal Escape

Some of the animals from Wild View Zoo have escaped. Each **sign** shows which **animal** should be inside each pen. **Colour** in the correct animal to return it to its pen.

That was zoo-per! Don't forget to give yourself a sticker.

Scavenger Hunt

Science

Tom has found some **objects** around his house.
Draw **lines** to match each object to the word that **describes** it.

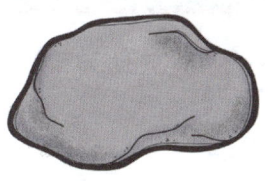   soft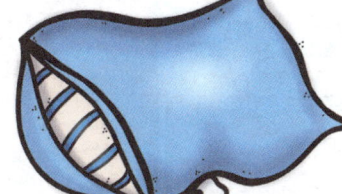

hard

   dull

bright

   smooth

fluffy

Now try this — It's time for your own **scavenger hunt**. Look around your **home**. Can you **find** something that is...

 long?   green?

 damp?   brown?

What did you find?

Great work! One last thing to hunt for — a sticker!

Summer Holidays — Week 6

Running Rhymes

Read the **poem**. Choose a word that **rhymes** with each **orange** word to complete the poem. Write your chosen words on the dotted lines.

I wait at the start,

Get set, then **run**.

Running quicker and quicker,

I have so much ....

| speed | fun | fear |

Choose the word that rhymes with 'run'.

My legs start to hurt,

And I long for my **dinner**.

I zoom to the end,

Will I be the .... ?

| winner | next | best |

Choose the word that rhymes with 'dinner'.

How many words can you think of that rhyme with 'run'?

Party Time!

Maths

The children have their **party hats** and **balloons** ready!

"Draw the right number of **balloons** in my hand to finish the pattern."

Write the **missing numbers** of dots to finish the pattern. Then **draw** the right number of dots on the blank party hats.

| 7 | | | 4 | | 2 | 1 |

Now try this — Give this present some **colourful** wrapping paper. Draw a pattern and colour it in.

Celebrate by giving yourself a sticker.

Summer Holidays — Week 6

Dino Matching

Can you draw lines to **match** each dinosaur to its **shadow**?
There is an **extra** shadow that doesn't match any of the dinosaurs. **Circle** it.

Roarsome work! Pick a sticker.

Handprint Fish

Week 6 Challenge

We're heading **under the sea** for this week's challenge. Careful — it could get a little **messy**!

What you need:

- Finger paints, including white
- A black felt tip pen
- Blue paper
- Googly eye (optional)

1. Choose a **colour** or colours for your fish. Paint your **hand** that colour with finger paint.

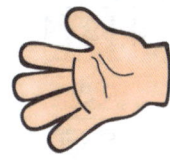

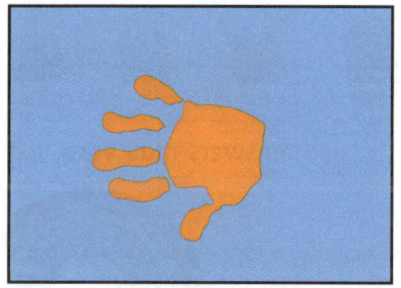

2. Gently **press** your hand onto the blue paper to make a print.

3. Use **white** finger paint on the tip of your **finger** to make **bubbles**. **Wait** for the paint to dry.

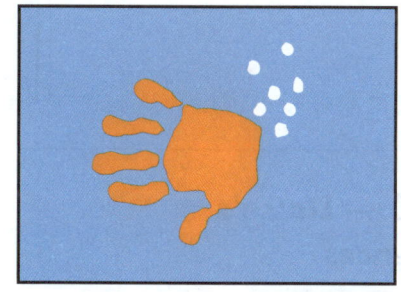

4. Use the black felt tip to add **details** to your picture. Draw on an **eye** (or stick on a googly eye if you have one) and a **mouth**, and any other details you like!

Summer Holidays — Week 6

Answers — Week 1

Page 2 — Camping Trip

Page 3 — A Walk Around Town

Page 4 — Wild Weather

Answers may vary, e.g.

Page 5 — Sounds on the Farm

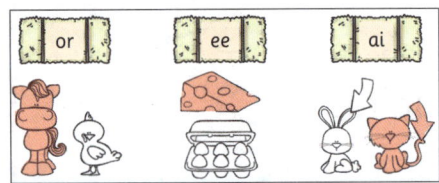

Page 6 — Shopping Trip

Page 7 — Colourful Combinations

Answers may vary, e.g.

Page 8 — Daisy's Differences

Answers — Week 2

Page 10 — Professor Pyramid

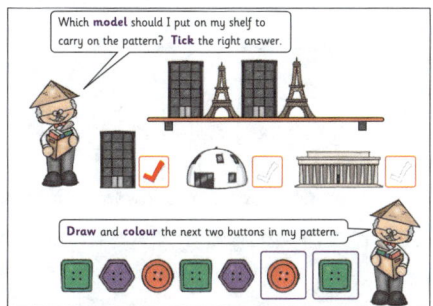

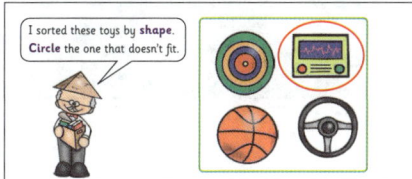

Page 11 — Animal Sounds

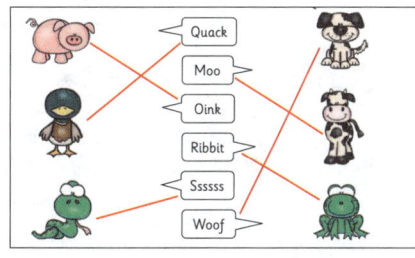

Answers may vary, e.g.

Page 12 — Lola's Loot

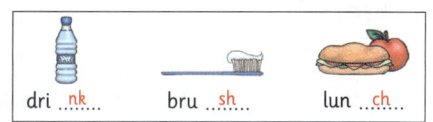

Page 13 — Brave Knights

Page 14 — Town or Country?

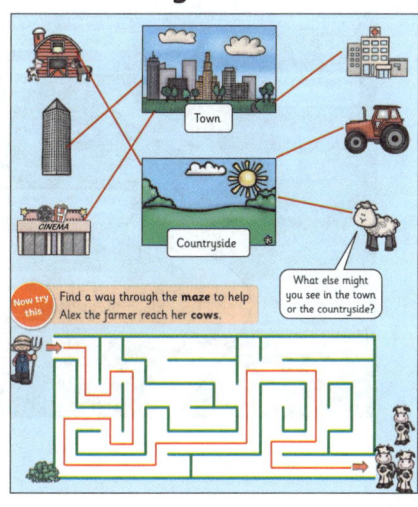

Page 15 — Fun at the Park

Page 16 — Alien Art

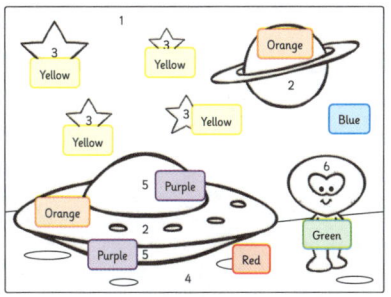

Summer Holidays — Answers

Answers — Week 3

Page 18 — Who Lives Here?

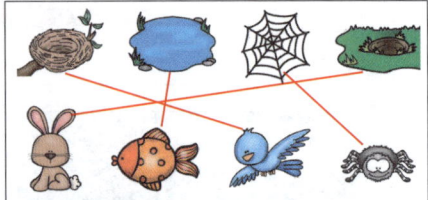

Page 19 — Make a Splash

Page 20 — The Flower Garden

Page 21 — Scenes from the Past

In the first picture you might have discussed:
- the market vs. how people buy food now
- the horse and cart vs. how people travel now
- the well vs. modern water supplies

In the second picture you might have discussed:
- the fire vs. central heating
- candles vs. electric lights

Page 22 — A Walk in the Park

Page 23 — Sweet Treats

Answers may vary, e.g.

Page 24 — Diving Dot-to-Dot

Answers — Week 4

Page 26 — Odds and Evens

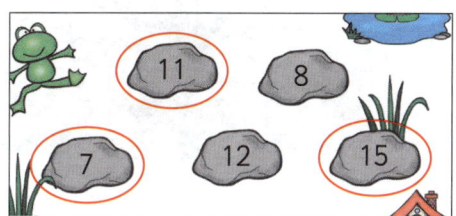

Page 27 — The Busy Bee

Page 30 — Arty Shapes

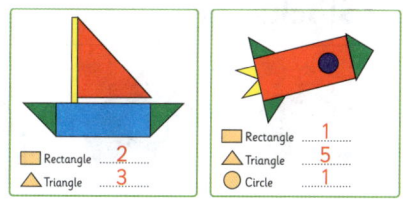

Answers may vary, e.g.

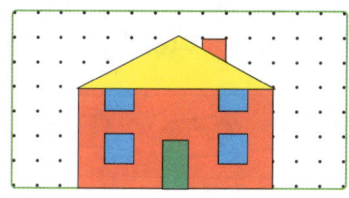

Page 31 — Sorting Toys

Page 32 — Different Places

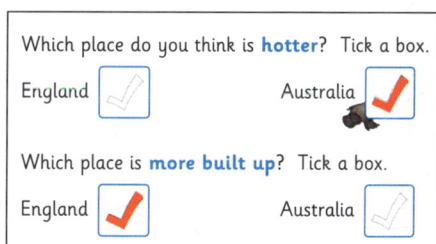

Page 33 — A Dog's Life

Page 34 — Find the Missing Piece

Summer Holidays — Answers

Answers — Week 5

Page 36 — Building Blocks

Page 37 — Ordering Pictures

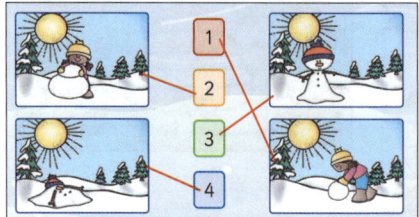

Page 38 — Colourful Creatures

Page 39 — Starry Sky

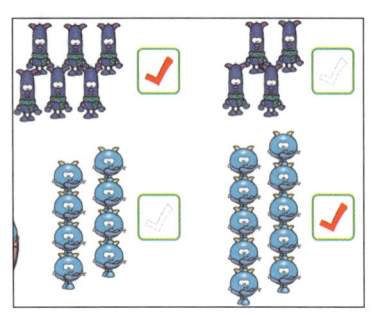

Page 40 — Playing at Gran's House

Page 41 — Toys Through Time

Answers may vary, e.g.

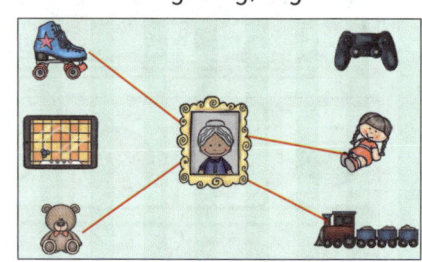

Page 42 — Pudding Patterns

Answers — Week 6

Page 44 — Season Scramble

Page 45 — How Many Raindrops?

Page 46 — Animal Escape

Page 47 — Scavenger Hunt

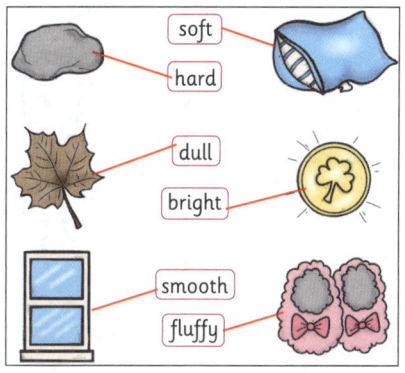

Answers may vary, e.g.

Page 48 — Running Rhymes

I have so much ..... fun ..... .

Will I be the ..... winner ..... ?

Other words that rhyme with 'run' include bun, done, won, sun and none.

Page 49 — Party Time!

Answers may vary, e.g.

Page 50 — Dino Matching

Summer Holidays — Answers 57

Summer Reading Challenge

Use this chart to keep track of the **books** you read this summer.
Fill in the **title** and **author**. Choose a **sticker** once you've finished the book.

Title	Author	Done!
		⭐
		⭐
		⭐
		⭐
		⭐
		⭐
		⭐
		⭐
		⭐
		⭐

Summer Holidays Superstar

Congratulations to _____

for completing their Summer Holidays Workbook!

Well done !

Signed _____

Date _____

My Summer Highlight

What was the **best bit** of your summer?
Draw a **picture** to show what you enjoyed most.

Write a **sentence** to describe what your picture shows.

....

....

Give yourself a sticker when you've finished each page.

Use these stickers on the progress chart in the middle of the book.